I0705646

The Myth of Racial Democracy

Restoring the African Mind Research Collection

Copyright © 2022 Restoring the African Mind Research Collection

All rights reserved.

ISBN: 9798365807587

1 BRAZIL: THE COMPLEX REALITIES OF RACIAL DEMOCRACY AND AFRICAN IDENTITY

"Because of the lack of a clear color distinction and a strong cultural tradition of tolerance and cordiality, as well as longstanding explicit laws against racial discrimination, Brazil has been touted as a 'racial democracy.' However, 'racial democracy' is a myth. There is a very strong correlation between light color and higher income, education, and social status. Few blacks reach positions of wealth, prestige, and power, except in the arts and sports."
-1997 Country Study of Brazil

"The black people feel in their flesh the lie that is racial democracy. You just have to look at the black families. Where do they live? The black children—how are they educated. You'll see that it's all a lie."
-Abdias do Nascimento

"In order to combat racism, it was necessary to prove its existence and to prove its existence it was necessary to demonstrate with figures the deep and persistent inequalities between blacks and whites that have been perpetuated through a number of mechanisms."
-Edna Roland

Brazil provides us with an interesting insight into the struggles of African people against slavery and racism, especially given the parallels one can draw with how Brazil has handled African people with that of the United States. Unlike how the United States has historically dealt with the issue of racism, Brazil has historically denied the existence of racism altogether. It is rather strange that Brazil was the last of the American colonies to abolish slavery, yet it was the first one to declare a racial democracy. Furthermore, Brazil seems to take pride in the fact that the segregation laws that existed in the United States never existed in Brazil. This is in fact true. Brazil did not see segregation as a solution to dealing black people, but rather they preferred to assimilate African people as a means to destroy them. They sought to "whiten" the African population as the following quotes shows:

> Now comes the necessity to devise some method of dealing with it [the Negro problem]. You of the United States are keeping the blacks as an entirely separate element, and you are not treating them in a way that fosters their self-respect. They will remain a menacing element in your civilization, permanent, and perhaps even after a while a growing element. With us the question tends to disappear, because the blacks themselves tend to disappear and become absorbed.

In Brazil there is a concept called "racial democracy," which suggests that people of all races are treated equally. This concept has been far removed from the reality of racism in Brazil, however. In an article entitled "Analysis: Brazil's 'racial democracy,'" Jan Rocha pointed out the fact that despite the large black population in Brazil, there are very few black people in government. The article reads:

> No other country outside Africa has such a
> large black population…yet blacks are almost
> totally absent from positions of power—from
> all levels of government, from congress, senate,
> the judiciary, the higher ranks of the civil
> service and the armed forces.

The article further points out that even up until the
1970s, carnival was exclusive to whites:

> And incredibly, up until the 1970s even
> Salvador's carnival parade was for whites—
> blacks could only push the floats, not dance
> around them. That situation only came to an
> end when a group of blacks set up their own
> black-only Carnival group, Ile Ayie, meaning
> big house in Yoruba.

Jan Rocha also references this attempt to "whiten"
Brazil:

> Most freed slaves were then turned out to
> become vagrants, homeless, jobless, penniless,
> while the authorities, alarmed that the majority
> of the population was now black or mixed race,
> did everything to encourage European
> immigration to "whiten" Brazil.

One of the key features of racial democracy was the
idea that the slavery was more humane in Brazil than it
was in other parts of the Americas. This was an idea
put forward by sociologist Gilberto Freyre. The reality
was that slavery in Brazil was extremely harsh. It was
a shorter trip from West Africa to Brazil than it was

from West Africa to the United States, so slave masters in Brazil were less hesitant to work their slaves to death because they could easily replace their slave population by importing more Africans. Hendrik Kraay explains: "Living and working conditions on sugar plantations were so harsh that slave populations failed to reproduce themselves and had to be sustained by imports." The number of slave revolts in Brazil alone is a testament to how unsatisfied enslaved Africans were with their treatment. Much like everywhere else that Africans were enslaved in the Americas, the enslaved Africans in Brazil constantly resisted their slave masters. Many times these slaves would escape and form separate maroon communities. The most famous of these maroon settlements was Palmares.

There were various other settlements created by escaped slaves, but Palmares stands out for its size and political organization. Palmares' economy was based on subsistence agriculture, trading, and raiding. Palmares was also a communalistic society, which was a direct contrast to the capitalistic economy of the Portuguese settlements. One spy reported that, "Everything was of all and nothing belonged to no one." Palmares also developed their own Creole language. Whites could only communicate with them through interpreters, although Zumbi spoke Portuguese and Latin, and could communicate directly with the Portuguese.

To obtain weapons and tools, the people of Palmares would raid nearby plantations. Afterwards, they began mining iron ore themselves. Though they could make iron tools and weapons, they could not make firearms. They did manage to obtain firearms as a tribute from white settlers that were allowed to live in Palmares, however.

There was a shortage of women in Palmares. To avoid fighting between men, women were permitted to have multiple husbands. The chiefs of Palmares were allowed to have multiple wives, however. Ganga Zumba had three wives; one mulatto woman and two black women. Zumbi may have also had multiple wives. Dandara is known to have been married to Zumbi, but some traditions state that Zumbi was married to a white woman named Maria. Women in Palmares were given a dominant status that they did not have in the Portuguese settlements. Whereas among the Portuguese, the men were the heads of the household, in Palmares it was women who were at the head of the household. Moreover, family relationships in Palmares were matrilineal, much as it was in many African societies.

Zumbi was the last of Palmares' chiefs and the most well-known. He was born in Palmares, but was stolen during a raid on Palmares in 1655 and raised by Catholic priests. He eventually made his way back to Palmares. There he would challenge Ganga Zumba for leadership. Zumba's leadership fell into question when, in 1677, an expedition led by Fernão Carrilho attacked Palmares. Many were killed or brought back to be enslaved. Zumba himself was wounded. The people of Palmares accused Zumba of being inept. Leading the plot to overthrow Zumba was Zumbi. Ganga Zumba later learned of the plot and he decided to make peace with the governor of Pernambuco. One of the terms of the treaty was that all runaways must be returned to the slave plantations. This treaty greatly concerned the people of Palmares, who did not wish to see their friends and family forced to return to the plantations.

Zumbi decided to strike. He managed to subdue all of Zumba's loyal followers and as a result the council named Zumbi as the new chief of Palmares. During the confusion that followed Zumbi's rise to power, Ganga Zumba was poisoned in 1680 by some of Zumbi's supporters. Zumba's plan was to form a treaty with the Portuguese so that he could live in peace, but Zumbi and many others did not trust the Portuguese and they believed the only way to maintain their freedom was to fight for it.

The final assault on Palmares began with Domingo Jorge Velho who led a 1,000 man attack. Zumbi and his soldiers were able to fend off the invasion. The governor of Pernambuco then sent Bernado Viera de Melo to reinforce the Portuguese troops, but they were once again defeated. Eventually, however, the Portuguese were able to take Macaco, the center of Palmares. During the raid, men were killed and women were captured. Captured mothers began killing their children so that the children would not be sold into slavery. The mothers would then starve themselves to death.

Zumbi was not found, however, and it was later revealed that he had escaped. Zumbi continued to raid for weapons to fight the Portuguese. One of Zumbi's lieutenants, a mulatto named Antonio Soares, was captured and tortured by the Portuguese. Initially he refused to give up Zumbi's position, but he agreed when the Portuguese promised him his freedom. Soares found Zumbi and stabbed him. Though he was wounded, Zumbi fought to the death. After he was killed, his body was mutilated. Zumbi's head was cut off and displayed by the governor of Pernambuco. Zumbi's legacy lived on, however. Many of his followers, who escaped the destruction of Palmares, continued to lead slaves to free maroon communities. These settlements remained hidden and unconquered. Many of them were not discovered until the 20th century.

An important figure during Zumbi's rule was his black wife Dandara. Although information on her is scarce, according to tradition, she was a warrior who fought for the liberation of slaves alongside her husband. She was also the mother of his three children; Motumbo, Harmódio and Aristogíton. Aside from her role as a warrior, Dandara also took care of sickly children and elders in the community. Like her husband, Dandara opposed Ganga Zumba's decision to sign a peace treaty with the Portuguese. She was fiercely committed to the fight against slavery. Her desire to be free was so great that when she was captured on February 6th, 1694 she killed herself rather than allowing herself to be taken into captivity.

Yet another major slave uprising in Brazil's history was the Malê Revolt in 1835. This revolt took place in Bahia, Brazil, making it one of the largest urban slave revolts in the history of the Americas. This event was also notable because it was African Muslims who were leading this uprising. One of the objectives of the revolt was to free an African Muslim named Pacifico Licutan, who had been jailed prior to the revolt. Licutan was a Muslim elder who was very well-respected by his followers. His followers had previously tried to buy Licutan's freedom on at least two occasions, but Licutan's master refused to sell him.

The 1835 revolt had actually been the culmination of a series of revolts in Bahia. There were also revolts in 1807, 1809, 1814, 1816, 1822, 1824, 1826, 1827,

1828, 1830, and 1831. The 1807 revolt took place during the government of Joao Saldanha da Gama, who was intolerant in his treatment of slaves and had enacted the systematic repression of maroon societies. The 1807 revolt was planned for the day of May 29th, but the conspiracy was exposed by another slave. The plan for the 1807 revolt was to seize ships to return to Africa. As a result of the 1807 plot, laws that prohibited Africans from holding religious assemblies were enacted.

There were also a high number of freed Africans living in Brazil, some of which were wealthy enough to own slaves of their own. By 1800 the number of free Africans in Brazil almost equaled the number of slaves. This was certainly an uneasy prospect for the slave owners who feared that the freed Africans would try to overturn the slave system altogether, as had happened previously in Haiti.

The case of Agostinho Jose Pereira is noteworthy because it revealed the fear that Brazilian society had about the possibility of a massive slave uprising. Agostinho Jose Pereira was a freeman and a religious leader who was jailed in 1846. Along with Agostinho were six other black men and six other black women, who referred to Agostinho as "Divine Teacher." Nine more of Agostinho's followers were also detained. The press speculated that Agostinho could have had as many as 300 followers. None of Agostinho's followers were slaves, and despite the fact that most whites in Brazil at the time did not know how to read, Agostinho and his followers were literate.

Agostinho was arrested on the suspicion that his sect was a front that was being used to plan a black uprising. The police were also concerned about a poem that was found in the possession of Agostinho's wife. The poem contained references to liberty and Haiti. They also found that Agostinho's personal Bible had highlighted passages that referred to liberty and the end of slavery. The court found Agostinho to be a very unusual figure. Not only was he a free black man who could read, but he had also taught his followers how to read. Agostinho, who was born to a slave mother in Recife, stated that his slave mother's mistress had taught him how to read. The court judges also laughed at Agostinho's claim to be divinely inspired by a holy vision. Agostinho was eventually released, as the court could find nothing to charge him with.

The poem regarding Haiti is a testament to the influence that Haiti had among the African population in Brazil. In 1824 a short lived rebellious new state named the Confederation of the Equator was formed. This Confederation was formed as a separate state, which was to be independent from the government of Pedro I. When Pedro sent a naval blockade to Recife, a large number of African people took to the streets in protest—on a side note, Agostinho was a military officer for the Confederation of the Equator. One of the protest songs that were sung by these African protestors was a reference to Henri Christophe, who was one of the major generals of the Haitian Revolution:

I will imitate Christophe

That immortal Haitian leader

Hurrah! We will imitate his people

Oh, my sovereign people!

The abolition of slavery in Brazil was a gradual process that served to prolong the institution of slavery. In 1871 the parliament enacted a law which stated that all children born to slaves were legally free. Despite being legally free, slave owners were still able to keep these children and use them for labor until they turned 21. Another law in 1884 freed slaves who reached the age of 60. Slavery was finally abolished in 1888 when Princess Isabel signed the "Golden Law." In doing so, Isabel finished the process of abolishing slavery, which was started by her father, Pedro II. Slavery was abolished, but many former slaves were still forced to work on the plantations for a small wage. Many other freed slaves found themselves being imprisoned in the newly built prisons. Unlike the United States, Brazil did not create bureaus to help improve the lives of the former slaves. In short, although slavery was over, the black population still lived restricted and impoverished lives.

Part of this notion of racial democracy is the concept of Brazil being very "mixed," but this so-called mixed heritage has always existed within the context of white supremacy. For this reason it was not uncommon that many mixed race people would choose to identify as "white" due to the social stigma that came with identifying as an African. Race and social status were so intertwined that in Brazil there arose a saying which stated that "money whitens." This idea of a black person becoming "whiter" through obtaining wealth and social status was also a factor in escaping from slavery. Chica da Silva is an example of this.

Chica da Silva escaped slavery through marrying

her white slave master. Together they had multiple children and when she died she was buried in a church that was exclusive to the white brotherhood. Though Silva was black, she dressed and acted like a white woman and in doing so she not only rose up the social ladder in Brazil, but she also amassed a great fortune. Her children followed in her footsteps, choosing to identify as white. Some of Chica da Silva's sons moved to Portugal with their father. They had to pay money to the Portuguese crown to have their black heritage erased from the records because one could not hold high positions in Portuguese society if they had black ancestry. Like their mother, they had to shed their black identity to advance socially.

This also has implications for the idea of racial democracy in Brazil. One can escape racial oppression, but only through denying their African heritage and embracing a European heritage—in this regard Brazil was no different from any other slave colony, or even the European colonies in Africa, where social mobility was largely based on embracing a European identity and disregarding African identity. Therefore, racial democracy was not based so much on equality between different races, but on the ability for African people to advance in a white dominated social hierarchy by becoming whites themselves. To some extent the same concept existed in the United States, in which it was beneficial for mixed race slaves to attempt to pass for white, although the distinction between blacks and whites in America was more stringently imposed. Larry Eugene Rivers gives the following description of how enslaved Africans attempted to escape their bondage by passing for white:

John Butler's assimilated black displayed a confident demeanor as he attempted to pass himself off as a white man. The owner claimed that this fair-skinned slave would present himself as free. Describing his runaway as a "yellowish" mulatto, the owner also noted that the fugitive would try "passing as a white man." Thomas Ledwith claimed that his slave Ned or Edward Dixon, a "bright quadroon," would attempt to "pass for a white man" because of his straight hair.

The other element of racial miscegenation is that it takes place within the context of black women being reduced to sex objects by the dominant white society. There is a famous saying in Brazil which goes, "white lady for marrying, black woman for working, mulatto woman for fornicating." This saying stemmed from the fact that white men often married white women, but had mulatto mistresses. Black women, who were not mulattos, were not even seen as being worthy enough for sexual objectification and were simply reduced to menial labor jobs. These views are not only held by whites in Brazil, as Bethan Rafferty points out: "It is common amongst Brazilians of African descent to encourage family members to have relationships with lighter skinned partners and be disapproving of darker skinned boyfriends and girlfriends." What we see here is that the black population has embraced the concept of "whitening" and often views their African identity as something negative.

One example that demonstrates the negative stigma associated with black identity in Brazil was when famed football star Ronaldo Nazário was questioned about the racism in European football stadiums. His response was: "I think that all blacks suffer (with racism). I, that am white, suffer because of so much ignorance." This statement was not only criticized by the black community in Brazil, but even Ronaldo's black father said, "he knows that he is black."

Vanessa Jesus Souza, a college student majoring in tourism, was among those who publicly commented on Ronaldo's statements. Souza's statements on the matter are interesting given that she looks white but chooses to identify herself as black because of her black grandparents. She stated: "I have fair skin, but my maternal and paternal grandparents are black, so I say that I'm black. My family came from the Northeast, my light eyes maybe a legacy of the Dutch heritage." This is not an association that others have accepted. Souza pointed out that her mother told her to stop referring to herself as black because she was white. Souza also noted that others mockingly call her "little black girl." Souza's situation also demonstrates a generational divide between her and her mother. In the wake of the Black Power movements in Brazil, it has become more commonplace to see people identifying with their African ancestry; even people like Souza that could pass for white. Whereas Souza's mother still holds on to notions of whitening and running away from one's African ancestry, Souza has embraced that identity. She has even gone beyond that, to identify herself as an advocate of affirmative action, so that blacks that are darker than she is can have the same type of opportunities that she enjoys.

The case of a Brazilian woman named Regiany offers a similar situation. Regiany, who has a white father, is very light-skinned. Despite this, she writes:

First of all, I was never white. But you will say this to those that always prefer to see in me only a thin nose, a white father, a *parda* (brown) mother and a very light-skinned sister with straight hair. They spent my whole life trying to convince me that my *parda* skin, of a light tone, would make me a *menina branca* (white girl), but I never accepted this.

Like Vanessa Jesus Souza, Regiany is aware of Brazil's attempt to whiten its African roots and consciously rejects this, explaining: "Sometimes I turn red in the sun and my nose is thin, but that doesn't mean that I'm not negra, this is what society prefers that I believe. It's easier to *embranquecer* (whiten) everybody and annul our African roots." Regiany also recounted how her own father would make racist remarks of "the worst taste." Regiany came of age and not only embraced her black identity, but has chosen to speak out against the "racism and the genocide of the black population." The stories of both women demonstrate that although "whitening" is a common occurrence in Brazil, many mixed race black people have chosen to do the opposite and identify with their African heritage.

One Afro-Brazilian activist that is worth mentioning in some detail is Edna Roland. During her many years of political activity in Brazil she has dealt with the complex and often intertwined issues of poverty, racism, colorism, and sexism. Roland has described her battle against racism as a fight against an invisible enemy because many people act as though the problem does not exist in Brazil. For this reason, much of Roland's fight against racism was simply to expose the existence of racism in Brazil and force the Brazilian government to acknowledge that racism.

Edna Roland was born in northeast Brazil, but migrated throughout Brazil for most of her childhood and adolescence. Roland grew up in a middle class family, which afforded her many opportunities. Her family also stressed the importance of education. At the age of 16, Roland left for the United States to study as an exchange student. It was there that she would discover her identity, as she explained:

> During a trip to the USA, I was in a bus with only white children and parked next to it was a bus with only black children. We heard a blast that sounded like a bomb, and the white students in my bus went into panic and then I realized that they were afraid because the other students were black. And I was also afraid of those black students, so I stopped to reflect…Who am I? What am I? And so I immediately began to question my own ethnic identity. In my childhood I had faced some discrimination within the family with relation to my white friends, but that did not raise my awareness. The moment of revelation was during that incident in the USA. It was exactly at that moment that I realized my own discrimination and racism, and begin asking questions about my identity.

It was during these years of military dictatorship that Roland became involved in political organizations when she joined the student movement. The military repression forced her to cut ties with her family, her university, and abandon her post-graduate studies. Throughout the 1970s Roland's actions were aimed towards the issue of the military government and the restoration of democracy in Brazil, but she eventually became involved in the fight for the rights of African people in Brazil.

The fight for African liberation gained some momentum in the 1940s and 1950s, with the creation of the Frente Negra Brasileira (Black Brazilian Front). Unfortunately this party was shut down by President Vargas, when he declared Brazil a one-party state and made all other political organizations illegal. With the restoration of democracy in 1985, a number of social movements began to reappear again. One of the black organizations to emerge during this period was the Unified Black Movement, (Movimento Negro Unificado) (MNU). In the early 1980s, Roland tried to get involved with the MNU, but was unsuccessful. Roland did become involved in the cultural aspects of the black movement in the '80s, however. She took part in African groups that paraded during carnival.

As mentioned before, Roland has described her fight against racism in Brazil as a fight against an invisible enemy due to the fact that the Brazilian government and the Brazilian people have often tried to ignore or downplay the existence of racism. Despite racism being an invisible enemy, it has had a very visible impact on the African community in Brazil. Roland explained in 1997 that there were more black people in college during the apartheid era in South Africa than there were in Brazil, which is one of the many shocking indicators of the low standards of living that Africans have had to endure in Brazil. Another indicator includes the poor healthcare offered to

Africans in Brazil.

Another issue is the way in which race is perceived in Brazil. Roland described race in Brazil as a type of continuum that goes from black to white—this continuum is so complex that it includes 134 different terms to identify blackness in Brazil. She further explained that a "person that might be considered black in one place, may be considered as brown in another or even white depending on the region of the country." Roland argued that this view of race was a "weapon" that was used against the black movement in Brazil because it helped to divide the black population. Roland explained: "People do not identify as belonging to the same group, you know, you have a number of different categories and people will not see as being a member of the same ethnic group, you know—so it's a very complex process." In fact, the lack of collective group identity has been one of the factors that have hindered black movements in Brazil.

Roland, who is herself very light-skinned and could, in some parts of the country, pass for white, has also been very critical in analyzing the concept of whitening in Brazil. As mentioned before, the concept of "whitening" was based on this idea that through racial mixing the African population in Brazil would eventually disappear. This goal has not been a completely successful one, as Roland points out, because one can say that the population was whitened, but one could just as easily argue that due to race mixing the population was also blackened. Of course, this mixture should also be seen in the context of white privilege and white supremacy in Brazil, in which very often mixed race people would identify as white simply because of the social status that comes with the white identity and the negative stigma of being African. As has been demonstrated, it was very often the case that mixed race children are encouraged by their own parents to deny their African heritage.

For Roland, and many other black women activists in Brazil, the struggle against racism has been entwined with the issue of sexism. In 1997, Roland became the president of Black Voice! This was an organization of black women fighting for the rights of the black population, with a specific emphasis on the rights of black women. What Roland and other black women activists have had to contend with was the reality that although black rights movements in Brazil fought against racism, there was sexism within those movements. Roland explained the struggles of black women in Brazil as follows:

> It was like this: the black woman was discriminated against three times, because she was black, because she was a woman and because she was poor. We lived the sum of these discriminations. It was an assertion that the black woman was the most discriminated against out of all women, because she suffered all of these conditions.

Roland's statements here are reminiscent of Malcolm X's statements about the way black women were treated in America: "The most disrespected person in America is the black woman. The most unprotected person in America is the black woman. The most neglected person in America is the black woman." For this reason Roland spoke of the necessity for black women to form organizations of their own, which was the purpose of the Geledes Institute of Black Woman, in which Roland served as Co-coordinator and Health Director. Roland explained:

> We, Geledés as a whole, the organization as a whole, emerged from our perception and from our consciousness of the necessity for an autonomous organization for black women. Because as long as we remained, whether within the black movement or even in mixed organizations-of men and women-or within the feminist movement (women's organizations), we were not able to get the attention [needed] for black women. Black women were always the last item on the agenda, whether for black men or for white women.

In 2001, Roland attended the World Conference on Racism, Racial Discrimination, Xenophobia and Related Intolerance in Durban, South Africa. On this occasion she was appointed as a speaker of the conference. In this capacity she, and other Brazilian activists, raised the issue of reparations for the descendants of enslaved Africans living outside of Africa. The conference also formed a consensus on using the term Afro-descendent to describe the descendants of enslaved Africans. Roland explained that "Durban was a watershed experience for the Brazilian Black Power Movement," because it was this meeting that forced the Brazilian government to revise its discourse on racial democracy. No longer could the government deny the existence of racism in Brazil after this conference. To demonstrate the extent to which the conference in South Africa changed the public discourse on race in Brazil, the Minister of Education Paulo Renato Souza wrote a letter addressing the topic of affirmative action; a topic which was previously considered taboo in Brazil.

Brazil, far from being a bastion of racial democracy, has been a nation where people of African descent have had to struggle for their rights. Despite being a majority in Brazil, African people are in a sense invisible. As this essay has demonstrated, African people are not proportionally represented in Brazil's government. African people also make up the poorest and most downtrodden elements in Brazilian society. Rather than eliminating racism, mixture has only helped to further confuse the issue of racism and to divide the black population. This mixture has also occurred within the context of Brazil's attempt to "whiten" the black population. Very often it is simply more advantageous for black people to try to assimilate into the white society and attempt to pass for white than it is for them to uphold their African roots and heritage. Despite these realities, there have been some organizations and activists (such as Edna Roland) that have challenged some of Brazil's racist policies and worked to expose "racial democracy" as being the myth that it is.

Selected References:

Andres Falconer, "The Black Voice: Edna Roland," The Synergos Institute, 2004.

Black Women of Brazil, "About colors and conflicts: My skin may be fair, but my soul is BLACK!," February 8, 2015.

___ "Brazil: The ideology of 'whitening' and the struggle for a black identity," February 9, 2012.

___ "Dandara, the wife of Zumbi, Brazil's greatest black leader, was a revolutionary warrior in her own right," November 20, 2014.

Bernd Reither, "A Genealogy of Black Organizing in Brazil"

Bethan Rafferty, "Is the high value placed on the beauty of mulatas in Brazil an example of Brazil's racial democracy or, in fact, an instance of its profound racism?"

"Brazil's Invisible Force," interview with Edna Roland, June 10th, 1997.

Cristiano Rodrigues & Marco Aurelio Prado, "A History of the Black Women's Movement in Brazil: Mobilization, Political Trajectory and Articulations with the State," *Social Movement Studies: Journal of Social, Cultural and Political Protest*, 12:2, 158-177, 2013.

Edna Roland, "The Economics of Racism: People of African Descent in Brazil," The International Council on Human Rights Policy, Seminar on the Economics of Racism Geneva, November 24-25, 2001.

Henry Louis Gates Jr., *Black in Latin America*, (New York and London: NYU Press, 2011).

Jan Rocha, "Analysis: Brazil's 'Racial Democracy,'

BBC News, April 19th, 2000.

João José Reis, "Slave Resistance in Brazil: Bahia, 1807-1835," *Luso-Brazilian Review*, Vol. 25, No. 1 (Summer, 1988), pp. 111-144

Kia Lilly Caldwell, *Negras in Brazil: Re-envisioning Black Women, Citizenship, and the Politics of Identity*

Larry Eugene Rivers, *Rebels and Runaways: Slave Resistance in Nineteenth-Century Florida*, (University of Illinois Press, 2012).

Mary Karasch, "Zumbi of Palmares: Challenging the Portuguese Colonial Order," *The Human Tradition in Latin America*, edited by Kenneth J. Andrien (Rowman & Littlefield, 2002).

Peter M. Beattie, editor, *The Human Tradition in Modern Brazil*, (Wilmington: Scholarly Resources Inc., 2004).

Rex A. Hudson, ed. *Brazil: A Country Study*. 1997.

Theodore Roosevelt, "Brazil and the Brazilians, *The American Missionary*, June, 1914.

2 SLAVERY AND RACE

Slavery was an important economic institution in the European settlement of the New World. Slavery provided a source of free labor for European planters in the New World. Out of the economic system of slavery came a social system based on race. This social system was designed to uphold the plantation economy by classifying labor and social relations based on race. Those who belonged to the white race occupied a position of power, whereas the black race was regulated to slavery. The aim of this essay is to explore the way that the concept of race not only shaped the development of the New World, but also how the idea of race impacted African people as well.

The slave trade not only helped to enrich Western societies, but it transformed the African societies which were impacted by the trade. It was observed that it was not unusual for a headman in Sierra Leone to have 200-300 slaves, while some of the Muslim rulers had between 700 and 1,000 inhabitants in their "slave towns." Walter Rodney noted that in most cases "their status was far removed from chattel slavery, but the fact remains that social relationships had been profoundly altered in the direction of disprivilege and unfreedom during the period of contact with Europeans, and the Atlantic slave trade bears the major share of the responsibility."

The wars in Africa helped to provide a supply of captives to be enslaved. An example of this is that the Mane would recruit some Sapes as captives, but sell as many as possible to keep the population manageable. Farma was a Mane ruler who died in 1606. It was noted that during his rule, it was not unusual to have twenty or thirty vessels loading slaves at any given time. The slave trade itself provided an incentive for such wars. It was reported by English slave traders in the 1580s that Farma would obtain hundreds of slaves on request by embarking on a campaign.

Wars of conquest were an aspect of the state formation process in Africa. These wars often produced a significant captive population. One example of this is the emergence of the Akwamu Kingdom. Under the rule of Ansa Sasraku, Akwamu engaged in a policy of imperial expansion. The result of this expansion was that Akwamu seized control of Great Accra. Akwamu also brought the Ladokou Kingdom under its control. The captives who were produced by Akwamu's military campaigns were marched to the state's capital district. There they would labor as slave cultivators. Some of the elite captives were ransomed, whereas others were ritualistically killed. Women captives in war were made to leave their homes to join the conquering group. They were assimilated as slave laborers and wives. War captives who were not absorbed into the existing slave population in Akwamu were led to the coast where they were sold. Little Popo was also known to be a warlike kingdom which engaged in the slave trade. Guns which were acquired from the slave trade helped to establish Little Popo as a military power in West Africa.

Stephanie Smallwood gave some idea of how the slave trade impacted African society. Smallwood argued that slavery and slave trading was likely already established throughout much of pre-colonial West Africa before the arrival of the Portuguese, but the arrival of the Portuguese transformed the existing slave trade. Smallwood explained: "The Portuguese had not introduced slave trading in African regions where no such commerce had existed prior to their arrival. But through the commerce they did introduce, they helped initiate a dramatic and abrupt shift in the scale of slave trading." This shift created "institutionalized markets for people" and reduced those people to commodities.

The extent to which there was an existing slave trade is difficult to ascertain. Forms of domestic slavery certainly existed in pre-colonial West Africa, but it does not appear that this was a universal practice. Walter Rodney noted that there were regions in Africa where absence of reference to any forms of local slavery would suggest an absence in the practice of slavery itself. What we do know is that the European presence incentivized slave trading. War captives who would otherwise be assimilated or killed now had commercial value and were sold to European buyers.

European traders themselves would incite conflicts for the purpose of increasing the number of captives which they purchased. The Bijagos were known as a fearsome group who engaged in raids which produced captives who were sold to European buyers. So brutal were the Bijagos that it was reported that they would set fire to the huts in a village and if the occupants came out fighting, they were cut to pieces. When European slavers found few or no slaves among the Bijagos, they would insist that the lack of slaves was a stain on the name of the Bijagos. These appeals to the honor of the Bijagos were done to incite them to bring more captives to be sold.

The Beafadas were among the groups who were attacked by the Bijagos, but the Beafadas themselves were engaged in slave raids. This demonstrated that the victims of the slave trade could just as easily be victimizers as well depending on the situation. Such conflicts were ultimately most beneficial to the European slave traders who acquired captives from these wars. The African ruling class and slave traders benefited in that they obtained European goods for selling captives to the Europeans. As a whole, however, the slave trade was destructive to African society. Rodney explained that the slave trade "proved entirely detrimental to African society, which was the weaker party." Indeed, slavery weakened African societies, while allowing Western nations to build profitable businesses and industries. An example of this is the role slavery played in the development of JP Morgan Chase.

The slave trade was detrimental for Africa because the wars to acquire the slaves were fought in Africa. As was already noted, even some of the groups which sold captives could themselves become victims of the slave trade. Whereas wars in Africa were fought over political power and control of wealth, the slave trade created an incentive to wage wars and engage in raids solely for the purpose of acquiring captives. This created a vicious cycle of war and instability which European traders and slave owners profited from. The more wars which were waged, the more slaves Europeans were able to acquire.

Apart from the economic ramifications of slavery and the slave trade, this historical event also had profound social implications. The enslavement of African people, as well as the subjugation of the indigenous population, resulted in the creation of a social structure of racism which placed white people above other races of people. Racism is also the reason why the European treatment of the captives which they bought differed from the African treatment of war captives. As was noted, captives who were not killed were assimilated into African societies. Within the racial societies of the New World, there was no hope for assimilation for African people who were considered to be an inferior people. Even those who became free were still limited by the fact that they were African.

Race as a social classification was of little prominence or significance in European and African societies prior to the colonization of the Americas. Ancient societies recognized that physical differences existed among humans from different regions of the world, but no political or economic significance was attached to these physical differences. This is not to suggest that forms of prejudice did not exist, but there was no institutionalized system of racism in Western society prior to the European colonization of the New World.

The system of white supremacy which Europeans constructed was one which varied from colonial society to colonial society. In the United States, for example, the one-drop rule developed as a means to classify anyone with a drop of African blood as being an African in the United States. This was not the case in countries such as Brazil or South Africa where mixed race individuals were treated differently than those who were black. The conception of white identity differed as well. For example, the Portuguese in Guyana were not regarded as being white because they came to Guyana as indentured laborers. White as an identity developed as one which was related to power. In colonial Guyana, the Portuguese did not have power as the British did, so they were not viewed as being white within that context. The Portuguese faced discrimination as well in Guyana because they did not fit into the construct of being white in Guyana.

Jews provide an interesting example of the concept of white identity in colonial societies. Jews were a group which had historically faced persecution in Europe for their religion. This persecution did not prevent Jews from participating as slave owners within the colonial economy, however. Some Jews also developed racist attitudes towards African people. This was a case in which a group which had been oppressed in Europe was in a position of power and dominance over African people, which further demonstrated the nature of racial hierarchy in colonial societies.

Jews were expelled from Spain in 1492 and were subsequently barred from settling in any of the new Spanish colonies in the Americas. Jews did settle in other parts of the Americas, however. Max J. Kohler noted that hundreds of Jews left Holland to settle in Brazil in 1624. Jewish settlers in Brazil came to make up the largest number of those who were transplanted from Holland, with the exception of those who worked for the Dutch West India Company. The Jewish settlers in Brazil worked as traders. The Dutch were forced to quit Brazil in 1654 after the Portuguese seized Pernambuco. Some of the Jewish settlers who left Brazil made their way to New York.

Slavery was a business in the New World and Jews were involved in that business. Kohler pointed out that "every New York family of any wealth or comfort held slaves, and in keeping and even in dealing in them the Jews were neither better nor worse than the Christian inhabitants." Kohler further explained that Jews in New York were involved in the slave trade as well.

Kohler found a record of "Simon the Jew" who was waiting for the arrival of his slave ship from Guinea.

Jews in the United States also displayed some of the discrimination towards African people which was typical of the era. Bertram Wallace Korn noted that "Jewish congregations would not accept Negro members." Korn further noted that the Charleston Beth Elohim constitution of 1820 accepted proselytes only if "he, she, or they are not people of colour."

Even though there were Jews who were slave owners and who engaged in discrimination against African Americans, Jews also continued to experience discrimination themselves. This exposed the complexity of the system of white supremacy. Though white Jews were white enough to find themselves in a position of dominance over African people, there were still segments within the white population which viewed Jews as outsiders and enemies. In Germany, the Nazis were so extreme in this view that they resorted to massacring the Jews.

Nazism itself arose out of the same racist logic which developed in the New World, which is why it is hardly surprising that the racist ideology of the Nazi regime was met with sympathy from racists in America. Madison Grant held the view that there would be an imminent racial conflict between whites and the non-white people of the world. Grant also criticized the wealthy classes for introducing African slaves and Asian immigrants to the detriment of common people. Lothrop Stoddard, who was influenced by Grant's work, was a proponent of eugenics. He also maintained a favorable view of the Nazi government in Germany.

In time, the United States found itself at war with

the Nazi regime in Germany. Even though the two nations were at war, there was still a mutual understanding that both nations were committed to the maintenance of white supremacy. This is demonstrated by the fact that German prisoners of war were treated better than African American soldiers were. The white supremacist ideology of the West was such that even though Western states clashed among each other over political power, there was still a sense of a shared racial identity.

David Walker, who was an American abolitionist, was one of the early critics of the white supremacist system which enslaved and brutalized African people. In his *Appeal*, Walker asserted that the disunity of Africans in the United States was the reason why they remained oppressed by white people: "Yea further, when I view that mighty son of Africa, Hannibal, one of the greatest generals of antiquity, who defeated and cut off so many thousands of the white Romans or murderers, and who carried his victorious arms, to the very gate of Rome, and I give it as my candid opinion, that had Carthage been well united and had given him good support, he would have carried that cruel and barbarous city by storm. But they were disunited, as the colored people are now, in the United States of America, the reason our natural enemies are enabled to keep their feet on our throats."

Walker's call for unity could be seen as an early example of what would come to be known as Pan-Africanism. Walker's book was addressed to the colored citizens of the world. He was writing not for an American audience alone, but for a global African audience. As the previous quote demonstrated, Walker also drew much inspiration from Hannibal's struggle against Rome. He saw Hannibal as an African warrior who was engaged in a war against a European foe, which was not unlike the situation of Africans during slavery who also confronted a struggle against European enslavers. Whether or not Hannibal was a black man is debatable, but Walker clearly identified with Hannibal because he saw a connection between Hannibal's fight against the Romans and the African American fight against American slave owners.

Walker believed that the Lord would give black people a Hannibal. He believed that this liberator which the Lord would provide to black people should be one who would receive support from his people. Walker was also clear in his view that there would be retribution for the suffering which white people inflicted on their slaves: "The whites want slaves, and want us for their slaves, but some of them will curse the day they ever saw us. As true as the sun ever shine in its meridian splendor, my colour will root some of them out of the very face of the earth. They shall have enough of making slaves of, and butchering, and murdering us in the manner which they have."

Walker also noted the brutality of slavery was such that the white slave masters prevented enslaved Africans from practicing the religion of Christianity. He stated: "The Pagans, Jews and Mahometans try to make proselytes to their religions, and whatever human beings adopt their religions, they extend to them their protection. But Christian Americans not only hinder their fellow creatures, the Africans, but thousands of them will *absolutely beat a coloured person nearly to death, if they catch him on his knees, supplicating the throne of grace.* This barbarous cruelty was by all the heathen nations of antiquity, and is by the Pagans, Jews and Mahometans of the present day, left entirely to Christian Americans to inflict on the Africans and their descendants that their cup which is nearly full may be completed."

The point that Walker made about religion is an important one for understanding race. The European slave masters were Christians, yet in their view race was a more important classification than religion was. Africans who converted to Christianity were not viewed as brothers and sisters in Christ by the European slave masters. For the Christian slave master on the plantations, Christianity became a tool to advance white supremacy.

Africans like Walker utilized religion for their own racial purposes. Whereas Europeans saw religion as a tool which helped to impose their dominance, Africans like Walker believed that the redemption of African people was divinely ordained. Walker was not alone in this view. Nat Turner's rebellion was premised on his belief that he was being divinely guided to rebel against slavery. Leonard Howell and Elijah Muhammad are other examples of this. This theological approach of viewing African people as chosen people of God was a reaction to the racial oppression which was inflicted on African people by white racists and has managed to inspire great acts of resistance on the part of oppressed black people.

Race has been so pervasive in Western societies that it has not only influenced religion, but politics as well. In the United States' political system, which has historically been dominated by two parties, we find that both parties may have ideological disagreements, but they both uphold white supremacy. Frances Butler Leigh wrote: "The Northerners take it for granted that every negro must be Republican, because the Republicans released them from bondage; they seem to forget that since the war the Republicans have really done nothing for the negroes, nor in any way fulfilled the many promises they made to them." Not only this, but Republicans were responsible for making a deal with Democrats in 1877 which gave the White House to the Republican, Rutherford Hayes. After a closely contested election in 1876, the two parties held a discussion in which the Democrats agreed to recognize Hayes as the president and Hayes in turn pulled federal troops from the South. This deal ended Reconstruction and restored Democratic control in the South. The deal was also a betrayal of the black people who supported the Republican Party.

President Hayes himself apparently did not think too highly of black people. George Campbell traveled to Washington on the same train with President Hayes and his wife. Based on his exchange with the president, Campbell wrote: "The President takes a very favourable view of the position and prospects of the negro. He thinks the present race of negroes are not equal to white men; but then, according to his views, the qualities of mankind are very much a matter of climate. Whether white or black, he thinks men are inferior in hot climates. The American blacks have not yet had time to develop higher human qualities nor to acquire much land, but he hopes they will."

In Campbell's view, President Hayes held a "favourable view" of black people, yet Hayes still believed that black people were not equal to white people. In Hayes' view, this was not based on an inherent inferiority. Hayes argued that this inferiority was the result of the climate, yet he still believed that there was inequality nevertheless. And this was regarded as being a "favourable view" of black people.

This inequality was further imposed through the criminal justice system. Marc Mauer explained: "The exclusion of felons from the body politic derived from the concept of 'civil death' that had its origins in medieval Europe. Such a designation meant that a lawbreaker had no legal status, and also had dishonor and incapacity imposed on his or her descendants. The concept was brought to North America by the English in the Colonial period. After the Revolution, some of the English common law heritage was rejected, but the voting disqualifications were maintained by many states." The purpose of this exclusion was to punish criminal offenders, but in the United States this policy took on a racial component given that America's anti-drug policies disproportionately targeted African Americans who were then disenfranchised and lost their ability to vote.

Mauer also noted that laws to prevent citizens from voting can be traced to the founding of the nation. Originally only wealthy white male property holders could vote. This excluded women, African Americans, and those who did not own property. Mauer noted that over time the barriers to voting were removed, with the exception of felons. This is due to the concept of "civil death" which was mentioned before. This has allowed for the continued disenfranchisement of African Americans. Mauer noted that in 2002 it was estimated that 13 percent of African American males were disenfranchised.

After the end of the Civil War, the South implemented a number of policies to prevent African Americans from being able to vote. This included a poll tax and literacy requirements. The situation was not much better in the North, where only six Northern states allowed African Americans the right to vote. Race was a fundamental aspect of the societies which developed out of the system of slavery in the New World and laws which restricted the voting rights of Africans were simply yet another one of the methods utilized to secure the dominant position of Europeans while keeping African people suppressed.

Selected References:

Adam J. Ondo, "Little Popo: The sociopolitical and economic erosion of a port town," 2014.

Bertram Wallace Korn, *Jews and Negro Slavery in The Old South 1789-1865*, 1961.

David Teather, "Bank Admits it owned slaves," *Guardian*, Jan. 21, 2005.

David Walker, *An Appeal to the Colored Citizens of the World*, 1830.

Marc Mauer, "Disenfranchisement: The Modern-Day Voting Rights Challenge," *Civil Rights Journal*, 2002.

Max Kohler, "Phases of Jewish Life in New York Before 1800," *Publications of the American Jewish Historical Society*, 1894, No. 2 (1894), pp.77-100

Sir George Campbell, *The American People or The Relations Between the White and the Black*, 1889.

Stephanie Smallwood, *Saltwater Slavery: A Middle Passage from Africa to American Diaspora*, (Harvard University Press, 2008).

Walter Rodney, *A History of the Upper Guinea Coast, 1545 to 1800*, (Oxford University Press, 1970).

3 FROM VARGAS TO MILITARY RULE IN BRAZIL

On September 4, 1942, about 40,000 public school students were assembled to pay homage to the "Brazilian Race." At the time, Brazil had just entered World War II to support the Allies. Jerry Davila noted the irony that this gathering "celebrated the Allied cause by imitating the public assemblies of fascist Europe." Such was the government of Getúlio Vargas, the man who was known as the "Father of the Poor." Vargas ruled as dictator from 1930 until 1934, then as elected president from 1934 until 1937, and then as dictator again from 1937 until 1945. He then served as a senator and was elected as president in 1951. Vargas' political career came to an end in 1954. Inflation and government debt reduced Vargas' popularity in the country. Faced with charges of corruption and demands from the military for him to resign, Vargas shot himself. He left a note which accused international and national forces of conspiring against his government.

Vargas' time in power saw significant transformations in Brazil. During the years that Vargas was in power, the armed forces were reorganized. This included placing the army in charge of Brazil's military police units. There were other significant shifts which took place under Vargas' leadership as well, such as the 1934 constitution which granted women's suffrage and created special courts to supervise elections. Vargas also oversaw the expansion of public education in Brazil.

Vargas was also an authoritarian figure who was known to co-opt, jail, or exile those who opposed him. Vargas' repressive measures hindered the fledgling black movement in Brazil. Vargas' policies forced the shutdown of the Black Brazilian Stand Up political party which was organized in defense of the black population.

Despite these changes, Vargas' government also maintained the racial inequality which existed in Brazilian society since the days of slavery. This included the limited employment opportunities which confronted black people. This is demonstrated by the career of a football player named Domingos da Guia. He represented Brazil on the international stage, but after he retired, he struggled to earn a decent living. A write-up in *The Human Tradition in Modern Brazil* explained: "While sports and music offered new opportunities to many Brazilians of African descent, the fruits of their labors were often ephemeral." What makes Brazil's situation unique is that all of this was carried out under the guise of racial democracy. This ideology was not based on the concept of racial inclusion, but rather a concept which was designed to render African descendants invisible, save for areas such as culture.

Vargas' policies were aimed at upholding this false notion of racial democracy. Vargas promoted Carnival parades as tourist attractions to showcase Brazil's African heritage, but this policy demonstrated a very superficial embrace of Brazil's African roots. Vargas wanted to give foreign dignitaries the impression that Brazil was a white nation, so he selected German immigrants for the presidential honor guard.

In the years which followed Vargas' death, political tensions in Brazil remained and eventually resulted in the establishment of a military dictatorship in 1964. There was a clash between those who sought to improve the conditions of the working class and the conservative elites who feared losing control of the state. These same elites had opposed Vargas because he wanted to use the state to improve the conditions of the lower class. These tensions were demonstrated by the life of Jôfre Corrêa Netto. Netto, who adopted the name "Captain Jôfre," rose to prominence in Brazil as a leader who fought for the rights of rural workers. Netto's date of birth is not known. Netto had given the date of his birth as April 3, 1921. He later began to assert that he was actually born in 1917, which appears to be an attempt on his part to associate his birth with the Bolshevik Revolution in Russia. Apart from his identification with the revolution in Russia, Netto dressed himself like Yasir Arafat of Palestine and Saddam Hussein of Iraq.

Netto followed the advice of his mother and joined the military in 1940, enlisting as a single, literate, white male. In 1939, Vargas implemented a mandatory military service law for men in Brazil. Those who were unable to document service in the military could not apply for government jobs, benefits, or register to vote. Fines were also given out to those who did not possess cards. Netto stated that he was introduced to the Communist Party while he was in the army, which is an interesting claim given that the armed forces in Brazil had been working to eradicate communist thought in its ranks. Netto served during World War II. After being expelled from the military in 1945, Netto worked a series of odd jobs and was arrested in 1953 for battery. In 1956, he was arrested again for knifing a man. This criminal record was later used to discredit Netto.

In 1959, Netto inspired tenant-farmers to uproot the

grass which they had planted in their crops. Netto found himself leading a struggle between tenant farmers and their landlords. This incident which became known as the "grass war" took place the same year as the Cuban Revolution. This led to Netto being labeled as the backland's Fidel Castro. In 1961, Netto himself had encouraged Brazilians to imitate Cuba's revolution. For his activities, Netto was arrested on multiple occasions. He was arrested in 1957. He was charged under a 1953 law which allowed for the "preventive imprisonment" of individuals who were deemed as a threat to the social order. Netto was arrested again in 1962. Netto was released in 1964, after the coup. Following his release, Netto was forced to deny any identification with the Communist Party.

The 1964 coup toppled the government of João Goulart. The military regime in Brazil remained in power until 1985. The transition from Vargas' government in the 1950s to military rule in the 1960s was a transition which took place in the context of class tensions, economic problems, and the inability by the political leaders of Brazil to address these tensions. These issues had existed under Vargas' leadership and Vargas himself took his own life after he lost control of the military.

Notes on sources:

Peter M. Beattie, editor, *The Human Tradition in Modern Brazil*, (Wilmington: Scholarly Resources Inc., 2004).

Rex A. Hudson, ed. *Brazil: A Country Study*. 1997.

4 RACE IN AMERICAN POLITICS

W.E.B. Du Bois stated: "The problem of the twentieth century is the problem of the color-line,—the relation of the darker to the lighter races of men in Asia and Africa, in America and the islands of the sea." Du Bois understood that racial discrimination had become the most serious problem of the twentieth century. It became so because of the position of power and dominance which white people maintained in the world. European nations set out to conquer and colonize the entire world. This gave birth to a philosophy which saw the white man as being racially superior to those whom he subjugated. The United States of America was one of the nations which was a product of this global racial imperialism.

America was created out of an act of rebellion against the colonial order which European nations created, yet America's birth was not a rejection of the racism which had justified the colonial ambitions of European nations. America rejected Britain's rule over a foreign colony, yet America had not rejected the idea that the white race was a superior race. David Brion David stated: "Even most history books fail to convey the extent that the American government was dominated by slaveholders and proslavery interests between the inaugurations of Presidents Washington and Lincoln. Partly because of the clause in the Constitution that gave the South added political representation for three-fifths of its slave population, Southern slaveholding presidents governed the nation for roughly 50 of those 72 years. And four of the six Northern presidents in that span catered to Southern proslavery policies. For example, Martin Van Buren, who came from a New York slaveholding family, sought to undermine the nation's judicial process and send the captives from the slave ship Amistad back to Cuba—and certain death. Millard Fillmore, also from New York, signed the Fugitive Slave Law of 1850, which enforced return of escaped slaves even from free states." This statement by David should give one some idea of how racist attitudes profoundly shaped the early decades of America's political history.

The problem of racism in American politics is a problem in which the basic human rights of African Americans have been denied by political leaders who have not viewed African Americans as equal human beings. There is an apparent inability to truly confront the extent to which racism has shaped American politics or how this racism has impacted the lives of African people. Joe Biden displayed this when he stated that Donald Trump was the first racist to be elected president in America. This is not true. Biden's remarks demonstrated the unwillingness to be honest about race in American politics and this unwillingness to confront racism has resulted in an analysis of America's political history which looks at presidents as individuals who are removed from the consequences of their policies. The racism of these presidents is often treated as a minor issue or often not even addressed at all. This can be demonstrated by remarks which Barack Obama made in an interview with AllAfrica. Obama stated: "I'd say I'm probably as knowledgeable about African history as anybody who's occupied my office. And I can give you chapter and verse on the—why the colonial maps that were drawn helped to spur on conflict, and the terms of trade that were uneven emerging out of colonialism."

Obama's response seems to ignore how racist some of the previous presidents were and how that racism impacted America's policy towards Africa. Some examples which come to mind are America's role in overthrowing Kwame Nkrumah, America's role in assassinating Patrice Lumumba, and America's support for apartheid in South Africa. The overthrow of Nkrumah is especially significant here because the interview with Obama was conducted ahead of his visit to Ghana. In the interview Obama also stated, "I'm a big believer that Africans are responsible for Africa." If he truly believed this, then why not allow Africa to handle the responsibility of the unrest in Libya, instead of intervening there? Obama was correct to point out that Africa is ultimately responsible for its own leadership, but it is disingenuous to speak of the issue of governance in Africa without acknowledging America's history of intervening in Africa's affairs.

The admiration which Franklin Roosevelt enjoys within the Democratic Party is yet another example of this point. When asked to name a political leader that they admire, both Hillary Clinton and Bernie Sanders named Roosevelt. Roosevelt is admired in American history for his New Deal policy which implemented government programs to assist impoverished Americans during the Great Depression. The problem with the New Deal is that it did not address the racial inequality in America. In the 1930s, the unemployment rate among African Americans was much higher than it was among white people. The policies of the New Deal not only failed to address racial inequality, but the manner in which the deal was implemented reflected these inequalities. For example, Social Security excluded African American men in certain occupations from its benefits. In response to the Social Security program, the *Crisis* stated: "Just as Mr. Roosevelt threw the Negro textile workers to the wolves in order to get the Cotton Textile code adopted in July of 1933 by exempting them from its provisions, so he and his advisors are preparing to dump overboard the majority of Negro workers in his security legislation program by exempting from pensions and job insurance all farmers, domestic, and casual labor." This is not to suggest that African Americans did not benefit from any of the provisions of the New Deal. The availability of low rent housing certainly did benefit African Americans, but the benefits were greatly hindered by the racial discrimination which African Americans faced. African Americans were the group that suffered the most during the Great Depression, but also received the least amount of help from the New Deal.

The African American community expressed other issues with Roosevelt as well. Roosevelt appointed Hugo Black to the Supreme Court, despite protests from the black community. Black was a former member of the Ku Klux Klan. Black initially refused to answer a question about his membership in the Klan, although Black later admitted that he was a member of the Klan and that he never rejoined the Klan after he resigned from the organization. Black wrote the majority opinion for *Korematsu v. United States*, which was a Supreme Court case that upheld Roosevelt's executive order in which citizens of Japanese ancestry were detained in "relocation centers." Black wrote: "Korematsu was not excluded from the Military Area because of hostility to him or his race. He was excluded because we are at war with the Japanese Empire, because the properly constituted military authorities feared an invasion of our West Coast and felt constrained to take proper security measures, because they decided that the military urgency of the situation demanded that all citizens of Japanese ancestry be segregated from the West Coast temporarily, and, finally, because Congress, reposing its confidence in this time of war in our military leaders—as inevitably it must—determined that they should have the power to do just this." Black stated that Korematsu was not excluded because of his race, but then specifically mentions the segregation of citizens of Japanese ancestry. Justice Roberts accurately noted that it was "the case of convicting a citizen as a punishment for not submitting to imprisonment in a concentration camp, based on his ancestry, and solely because of his ancestry, without evidence or inquiry concerning his loyalty and good disposition towards the United States."

There was also the problem of anti-lynching legislation. Roosevelt refused to commit to supporting anti-lynching legislation. The reason for this was political. The Democratic Party included senators who outright opposed laws banning lynching, such as Huey Long. Long argued that such a law would actually harm black people. Senators Pat Harrison and Ellison Smith saw the anti-lynching legislation as a threat to white civilization, southern women, and the Democratic Party. Roosevelt admitted: "If I come out for the anti-lynching bill now, they will block every bill I ask Congress to pass to keep America from collapsing. I just can't take that risk." *The Crisis* reported that Roosevelt was willing to "spend billions to keep people from relief rolls, but is unwilling to say one word to prevent his fellowmen from being murdered by mobs."

There was a decrease in lynching activity in 1935 when the anti-lynching bill was being debated, but after the bill was defeated in Congress there was an increase in lynching. Roosevelt was content to remain silent on the matter. He was content to allow black people to be lynched, so long as he did not risk losing the support of Congressmen in the south. This silence on the matter resulted in a group of black women picketing the National Democratic Headquarters in New York City to condemn Roosevelt's silence. Rexford Tugwell stated that "Franklin had watched the fight, but had not intervened. He had been urged again and again to exert his leadership, but he had turned his back."

Roosevelt would not risk alienating a portion of the Democratic Party by offering public support for anti-lynching laws. The unwillingness of Democratic presidents to forcefully challenge racism in America would continue in the years that followed. Take for example Lyndon B. Johnson. As Obama pointed out, for the first twenty years that Johnson was a senator, he had opposed civil rights legislation. Johnson did support civil rights legislation once he became president, yet Johnson was also the same man who sided with segregationists in Mississippi against the Mississippi Freedom Democratic Party. Much like Roosevelt, Johnson would not risk alienating southern segregationists within the Democratic Party. Of course, Obama did not mention this aspect of Johnson's politics. Obama merely stated that Johnson was "not a perfect man." The issue is not whether Johnson was perfect or imperfect. The issue is how Johnson's policies impacted African Americans. One cannot deny that Johnson did sign important civil rights legislation into law, but his unwillingness to challenge racism within his own party had the effect of ultimately undermining civil rights in America.

The Republican Party provides more examples of racism on the part of an American president. Richard Nixon was infamously forced to resign following the Watergate scandal in which burglars broke into the office of the Democratic National Committee. Nixon lied about not being involved in the attempt to cover up the break-in. Following Nixon's resignation, Gerald Ford was sworn in as president and Ford pardoned Nixon. Nixon was also a racist. Nixon's views on black people were summed up by H.R. Haldeman, who noted that Nixon expressed the view "that there has never in history been an adequate black nation—and they are the only race of which this is true. Says Africa is hopeless—and the worst there is Liberia, which we built." In a recorded exchange between Nixon and Ronald Reagan, Nixon was heard laughing after Reagan referred to African leaders as monkeys.

Reagan's administration was marked by several scandals such as "Debategate" in which documents from the campaign of Jimmy Carter were illegally transmitted to Reagan's team. A much larger scandal was the Contra scandal. This scandal involved a deal made between Iran and the American government in which the American government sold missiles to Iran, which was a violation of the arms embargo which was in place. The deal secured the release of American hostages who were being held hostage. The funds which were acquired through the sale were used to finance the Contras who were fighting against the government in Nicaragua. Reagan also provided CIA assistance in supporting the UNITA rebels in Angola. Nixon and Reagan were two racists who oversaw scandal ridden presidencies. Nixon felt that Africans never had an adequate country and Reagan saw Africans as monkeys. Obama's claim to have the same level of knowledge about Africa's history as men such as Nixon and Reagan was hardly reassuring.

The racism of American political leaders has often posed a challenge for African Americans, who have struggled to engage in the political system in a manner which can truly advance their interests. W.E.B. Du Bois provides an example of this. Du Bois stated that he "espoused the cause of Woodrow Wilson" and even went so far as to resign from the Socialist Party which he joined to avoid being disciplined for not voting for the Socialist ticket. He explained: "I could not let Negroes throw away votes." He wrote: "We sincerely believe that even in the face of promises disconcertingly vague, and in the face of the solid caste-ridden South, it is better to elect Woodrow Wilson President of the United States and prove once for all if the Democratic Party dares to be democratic when it comes to black men. It has proven that it can be in many Northern states and cities. Can it be in the nation? We hope so, and we are willing to risk a trial."

Du Bois noted that after Wilson was elected, he proceeded "to segregate nearly all of the colored Federal employees, of whom there were a considerable number, herding them so far as possible in separate rooms with separate eating and toilet facilities." William Monroe Trotter was dismissed by President Wilson when Trotter attempted to lead a delegation to protest the president's segregationist policies.

Du Bois explained that black people found themselves politically helpless in 1916 and there was little choice but to vote for Wilson. In 1912, Du Bois had supported Theodore Roosevelt and the Progressive Party, otherwise known as the "Bull Moose" movement. He saw this as an opportunity to develop a third party. Du Bois wrote a proposed plank for the Progressive Party. The plank stated: "The party, therefore, demands for the Americans of Negro descent the repeal of unfair discriminatory laws and the right to vote on the same terms on which other citizens vote." Roosevelt wanted nothing to do with Du Bois, whom he described as a "dangerous" person. The Progressive Party would not even seat most of the black delegates at its convention.

Smaller parties have offered a platform for political figures who would otherwise be unable to find a platform within the Democratic or Republican parties. An example of this is the fact that Clifton DeBerry was able to secure the nomination of the Socialist Workers Party in 1964. DeBerry was nominated again in 1980. In the 1964 campaign, DeBerry identified unemployment and civil rights as the chief domestic issues in America. He also described the Republican and Democratic parties as "the two cold-war, big business parties". Third parties have not been innocent of racism, however. The struggles which Claudia Jones experienced within the Communist Party demonstrated this.

Jones was born in Trinidad in 1915. Her family migrated to New York in 1922. Jones eventually became active in the National Urban League. The event which exposed Jones to the Communist Party was the Scottsboro Nine case in 1931. Nine black boys were accused of raping two white prostitutes. They were tried without an attorney. The Communist Party intervened to support the nine boys through the

International Labor Defense group. After several years, the nine were found not guilty and were released.

Jones joined the Young Communist League in 1936. By 1941, she became the National Director of the Youth Communist League. Jones' position in the party did little to attract support from the black community. Connie Johnson explained: "Despite her position as one of the few African-American women in a leadership position within the CP, Jones did not have tremendous success in converting large numbers of black men or women to Communism. This, in part, may have had more to do with fear of Jim Crow brutality and retaliation if caught engaged with the CP than an unwillingness to consider the merits of social change or equality." The racism of white socialists was also a significant factor in why black people avoided engaging with the CP.

Jones' work within the Communist Party also made her a target of the American government. She was deported to Britain in 1955. In Britain, Jones encountered the racism of the British Communist Party. Jones believed that white communist workers had "a special responsibility" to support black women's autonomous struggles because "they inevitably resisted race, class, and gender exploitation and thereby took aim against the whole capitalist system." The problem that Jones experienced was that some of her white communist comrades did not believe that they held such a responsibility towards black women. Jones died in Britain at the age of 49. Johnson summed up Jones' struggle within the Communist Party as follows: "Jones obviously felt that African-Americans were members of an oppressed group whose salvation was firmly rooted in Marx's

Communism. That Jones would be forced to fight for support and approval within the Communist Party itself is certainly painful and ironic. Although Jones' efforts and commitment to the Party would prove to be a bittersweet victory during her lifetime, one can only hope that she found some consolation in the final pay-off at death: a gravesite next to that of Karl Marx."

Where matters of race are concerned, third parties have often not been much different than Democrats or Republicans. This was a point made by Marcus Garvey when he stated that "socialism is only another form of white control that the white man is going to fasten around the neck of the Negro peoples of the world." Garvey further declared: "Before you can accept socialism as a cure, you have to change the white man's soul; and that, the Negro socialists have not done yet." Garvey also stated that the socialist "is the same Republican, the same Democrat as other white men." By this, Garvey meant that socialists were just as racist as Republicans and Democrats were. This merely demonstrates just how pervasive the problem of racism in American politics has been. Even political parties that have presented themselves as alternatives to the two major parties have also displayed racism towards African Americans.

Selected References:

Connie Johnson, "Reclaiming Claudia Jones: When a Black Feminist Marxist Defies McCarthysim" *Michigan Feminist Studies*

Earlene Kelly Parr, "Franklin D. Roosevelt and the Negro in the 1930's," 1965.

Fred Halstead, "Socialist Workers Party Nominates DeBerry as Candidate for President," *The Militant*, January 13, 1964.

Federal Election Commission October 22, 1980.

Marcus Garvey, *Selected Speeches and Writings of Marcus Garvey*, (Dover Publications, 2005).

Peter Scott Dale, "Contragate: Reagan, Foreign Money, and the Contra Deal," *Crime and Social Justice*, 1987.

Remarks by the President at LBJ Presidential Library Civil Rights Summit, April 10, 2014.

Stephen E. Ambrose, "Why Didn't Nixon Burn the Tapes and Other Questions About Watergate," *Nova Law Review*, Volume 18, Issue 3, 1994.

5 BROTHERHOOD OF THE BOAT

Brother Marvin's song "Jahaji Bhai" sought to bring about a feeling of racial unity in Trinidad, but his attempt to foster this unity was done at the expense of placing the particular cultural and historical experiences of Indian people above the experiences of African people. For example, the very title of Brother Mavin's song invokes the experiences of Indians who came to Trinidad via ships. The term "jahaji bhai" is a Hindi phrase which means brotherhood of the boat. It referred to the sense of brotherhood among the Indians who came to Trinidad as indentured laborers. Brother Marvin attempted to expand this concept to one which includes Africans who also arrived in Trinidad in ships.

In the song Brother Marvin states "our ancestors came by boat." This is true, but in making such a statement Brother Marvin was simplifying history in a way that is dismissive of the struggles which African people endured. It is true that Europeans, Africans, and Indians all arrived in the Americas on ships, but not all of these journeys were the same. Malcolm X had stated that African Americans did not arrive in the *Mayflower* and that their ancestors were not the pilgrims. The Africans who arrived in Trinidad arrived in slave ships, which is a much different experience than the experience which Indians had on their journey to Trinidad.

Black Stalin's song "Caribbean Unity" was a controversial song for its exclusion of Indians and other racial groups in the Caribbean, but Black Stalin did speak to the shared experiences of African people who endured the same hellish condition on the slave ships. This is not an experience that Indians endured in their journey to Trinidad. It is also important to note that Brother Marvin specifically mentions *Fatel Rozack*, but he does not refer to any particular slave ship. This is an example of the fact that Brother Marvin treats the Indian experience in very specific terms, but he does not give the African experience in Trinidad the same type of treatment. This is an issue that one notices throughout Brother Marvin's song. For example, Brother Marvin describes himself as being "part seed of India", but says little of his connection to Africa in his song.

Brother Marvin explained that his bahut ajah (great grandfather) was from Calcutta. Brother Marvin intones:

> The indentureship and the slavery
> Bind together two races in unity
> (Achcha dosti)
> There was no more Mother Africa
> No more Mother India
> Just Mother Trini
> (Janmabhoomi)
> My bahut ajah planted sugarcane
> Down in the Caroni plain
> So Ramlogan, Basdeo, Prakash, and I
> Is jahaji bhai

Brother Marvin explained that without his great grandfather he would not have zindagee (life). Brother Marvin intimately describes his connection to his Indian ancestry and other Indians, but he has much less to say about his connection with Africa. Brother Marvin states that he considered it a "great privilege" to be fifty percent African and fifty percent Indian, but beyond his expressed pride in his African ancestry, Brother Marvin has little to actually say about his African ancestors and his connection to African people in his song. Instead, he seems to chastise those who claim to be true African descendants for not recognizing that they may have Indian ancestry as well:

> For those who playing ignorant
> Talking 'bout true African descendant
> If yuh want to know de truth
> Take a trip back to yuh roots
> And somewhere on that journey
> Yuh go see a man in a dhoti
> Saying he prayers in front of a jhandi

It is rather revealing that Brother Marvin would choose to specifically address those who claim to be true African descendants, but he says nothing to Indians. Brother Marvin does not invite Indians in Trinidad to consider the possibility that they may have some distant African ancestry. Brother Marvin also does not refer to Indians as being "ignorant" for claiming their Indian ancestry. Finally, Brother Marvin seems to be trying to present himself as being more informed and enlightened than the "ignorant" individuals who claim to be African descendants because he is aware of his Indian ancestry and takes pride in it. He does not seem to consider that there are African descendants who are aware that their roots are comprised of Indian ancestors, yet still proudly claim to be descendants of Africa.

Brother Marvin's calypso invoked a response from Sugar Aloes, titled "Unity." Sugar Aloes' response was not only aimed at Brother Mavin, but also at the United

Congress (UNC) government of Trinidad and Sat Maharaj, who is a Hindu religious leader. Sugar Aloes begins by singing:

Unity
My PM ask me for unity
It's a lovely request
But who the hell he trying to fool

Throughout the song Sugar Aloes points out that the cultural exchange in Trinidad is, in his view, not an equal one, as many Indians often refuse to participate in African cultural celebrations. For example, Sugar Aloes sings: "When I keep Shango feast and they come by me, then I go believe they ready for unity." Sugar Aloes also points out that slavery and indentureship were different experiences because unlike Indians, Africans were brought to Trinidad by force. He acknowledges that Indians and Africans were oppressed by the white man, but Sugar Aloes also points out that the oppression of the two groups was not the same.

In response to Brother Marvin's remark about ignorant African descendants, Sugar Aloes intones:

For a few penny
He desecrate African history
Then try to mamaguy we
Saying he promoting unity
He proclaim to be so proud to be part seed of India
He big up he grandma and pa
But I was ignorant
To claim African descendant

Sugar Aloes suggests that Brother Marvin was allowing himself to be used by Indians. Sugar Aloes notes that despite all of the love that Brother Marvin received from the Indian community for his song, Brother Marvin came third to last in the chutney contest. Sugar Aloes sings:

> Big chutney contest
> I prove him to be an ass
> When the judges said he came third to last
> All the love they love he "Jahaji Bhai"
> He still couldn't defeat Sonny Mann nor Rickey Jai
> But in the Dimanche Gras competition
> They found that Brother Marvin got robbed
> They never see Cro Cro as the champion

Despite this, as Sugar Aloes notes, Brother Marvin was embraced by Sat Maharaj. Sat Maharaj allegedly stated that he would never have grandchildren if his daughter married a black man. By associating himself with Sat Maharaj, Sugar Aloes seems to be suggesting that Brother Marvin undermined his own message of national unity. Sugar Aloes also notes that even though it was Cro Cro who won the calypso monarch at the Dimanche Gras competition, Sat Maharaj decided to honor Brother Marvin by placing a garland around his neck. Here Sugar Aloes is pointing out that though Brother Marvin ranked very low in the chutney competition, Sat Maharaj seemed to have embraced Brother Marvin solely to express his dissatisfaction with Cro Cro winning the monarchy.

Sugar Aloes also calls on Prime Minister Badeo Panday to address Sat Maharaj's racialism. Sugar

Aloes reminds Panday that if it wasn't for "two jackass African" Panday would never be prime minister of Trinidad. This was a reference to the fact that the UNC won the 1995 election after forming a coalition with the National Alliance for Reconciliation (NAR), which only had two seats. The coalition between the two parties was enough to unseat the ruling People's National Movement (PNM) political party. Here Sugar Aloes is expressing his clear displeasure with the two Africans who decided to join with the UNC, allowing Panday to become prime minister.

Brother Marvin also sings that there is no more Mother Africa or Mother India, only Mother Trinidad. In saying this, Brother Marvin invoked a similar sentiment that was expressed by Eric Williams, who wrote: "There can be no Mother Africa for those of African origin, and the Trinidad and Tobago society is living a lie and heading for trouble if it seeks to create the impression or to allow others to act under the delusion that Trinidad and Tobago is an African society." In "We Is We," Chalkdust had expressed a similar view when he chastised young people in Trinidad who were looking to India and Africa for their identity.

In "We Is We," Chalkdust described the afro (or as Chalkdusts says "fathead") and dashiki wearing youths as being "color crazy" for wanting to know more about Africa. In that song Chalkdust claims that he is not condemning Africa, but he also employs some very negative and stereotypical views of Africa. Chalkdust sings: "We have no tribal wars down here/We don't know about tom-tom and spear." Chalkdust also suggests that Trinidadians should never view African American artists such as Otis Redding as heroes, which is also contrary to the spirit of global African unity which Garvey tried to foster. What is especially interesting is that in "We Is We," Chalkdust sings that only Trinidadians "know about obeah man."

I reference Chalkdust specifically because he was someone who opposed the growing interest in Africa and instead told the youth in Trinidad that they would find their identity in Trinidad, yet Chalkdust would also become a prominent voice promoting African identity and unity in the Caribbean. In "Why Milo," for example, Chalkdust spoke of a common culture in the Caribbean which was rooted in Africa:

> Our music, yes our culture
> Common experiences they share
> Some may sound different, but their roots are in Africa
> The Bongo and your Bamboula
> Were danced on all plantations here

The reality is that Africans in Trinidad and Tobago share a cultural and historical connection to Africa and to Africans in other parts of the Diaspora. Being enslaved in the Caribbean did not eliminate this connection to "Mother Africa". This is why Chalkdust, who once told young people who were interested in Africa "that is right here [in Trinidad] you will find your identity", would also explain:

> You don't have to go by plane to Ghana
> In order to see Africa
> Every time you pound plantain with mortar and pestle
> Or on your hand you wear your slave band

Or when the moko jumbie walk talk amidst the
people
Then you rubbing shoulders with Africans
Understand

Chalkdust came to understand that the African roots
of the African descendants in Trinidad was not
something which could be easily dismissed because the
cultural connection to Africa still remained. It was to
be found in the very artform of calypso itself.
Chalkdust explained that the main elements of
calypso—such as the call and response, calypso's
sixteen bars, and satire in calypso—are all part of the
griot tradition of Africa. During one of his lectures,
Chalkdust was informed by a young man in the
audience that kaiso (another term for calypso) was an
Igbo word. The connection between calypso and the
music of Africa was also apparent when Lord Pretender
and Lord Kitchener from Trinidad met with Koo Nimo
who is from Ghana. Koo Nimo informed the two
calypsonians that calypso has rhythms which are very
similar to the highlife music which Koo Nimo
performs. As it turned out, Lord Kitchener liked
highlife music very much.

The aim of Brother Marvin's song was to address
the existing racial tensions in Trinidad. The origin of
this racial tension can be traced to the British colonial
period. Enslaved Africans were brought to Trinidad in
the 18th and early 19th centuries to work on sugar,
cocoa, and coffee plantations. The institution of slavery
created a rigid racial hierarchy that placed whites at the
top and Africans at the bottom, fostering deep social
and economic inequalities. When slavery was
abolished in 1834, formerly enslaved Africans sought

to assert their freedom by leaving the plantations and forming independent villages. Many refused to return to the plantation system that symbolized their oppression.

Faced with a labor shortage, British planters turned to India as a new source of cheap labor. Beginning in 1845, tens of thousands of Indians were brought to Trinidad under the indentureship system. This system lasted until 1917. Indians were bound by contract to work for fixed terms under harsh conditions. Unlike Africans, who were considered free citizens after emancipation, Indians were treated as temporary laborers and were often isolated in rural estates. This separation created a dual society in which Africans and Indians developed distinct cultural and economic spaces with limited interaction.

As they did with Africans who were used as slave labor, the Europeans also came to view Indians as being an inferior people who were fit for servitude. Lord Harris, the Governor of Trinidad, declared of both Africans and Indians: "The only independence which they would desire is idleness, according to their different tastes in the enjoyment of it; and the higher motives which actuate the European labourer […]." Given the negative views of Indians, it is not surprising that the Indian laborers were treated very harshly by the plantation system. From 1909 to 1912, there were nearly 8,000 cases of Indians in Trinidad being prosecuted. The main offense that was committed was desertion. Other offenses included being absent from work without a lawful excuse or not finishing work. Vagrancy was a crime that was punishable by the law. Laws concerning Indians restricted their freedom of movement and ensured that they remained on the plantations.

The wages that the Indians received was a mere pittance of the massive amount of the wealth that the plantation managers received from Indian labor. In British Guiana, in 1912, the average weekly earnings of an indentured laborer were $1.23 in Demerara and Berbice. It was slightly less in Essequibo, being $1.14. Indians also had to endure terrible living conditions on the plantations. A memorandum that was submitted by Mr. Lechmere Guppy to the Royal Franchise Commission of 1888 exposed what living conditions were like for Indians in Trinidad:

> As first in the list of evils which afflict the Colony, I look upon the system of housing the Indian Immigrants in barracks. It was not introduced until after Major Fagan had been dismissed and the subjugation of the coolie to a five years' indenture to a master imposed upon him by the Government had become complete. At the outset barracks were only built for the Indians who came unaccompanied by women, and free labourers were lodged as before in separate cottages. The first in Naparima was erected at Palmyra Estate, and I think that one was the first in the Island: but as the estates got fully supplied with coolies the cheapness of the barrack caused it to be adopted universally. The barrack is a long wooden building eleven or twelve feet wide, containing perhaps eight or ten small rooms divided from each other by wooden partitions not reaching to the roof. The roof is of galvanised iron, without any ceiling; and the heat of the sun by day and the cold by

night take full effect upon the occupants. By standing on a box the occupant of one room can look over the partition into the adjoining one, and can easily climb over. A family has a single room in which to bring up their boys and girls if they have children. All noises and talking and smells pass through the open space from one end of the barrack to the other. There are no places for cooking, no latrines. The men and women, boys and girls, go together into the canes or bush when nature requires. Comfort, privacy and decency are impossible under such conditions. A number of these barracks are grouped together close to the dwelling house of the overseers, in order that they may with the least trouble put them out to work before daylight in crop time, which they do by entering their room and, if necessary, pulling them off their beds where they are lying with their wives. If a man is sick he is not allowed to be nursed by his wife, he must perforce go to the hospital far away, leaving his wife, perhaps without the means of subsistence, in such a room as I have described, to her own devices, amid the temptations surrounding her. With all this, can any one wonder at the frequent wife-murders and general demoralisation amongst the Indian immigrants? In fact the barrack life is one approaching to promiscuous intercourse. And the evil is not confined to the coolies. No decent black labourer can take his wife to live amongst such surroundings. For very long past I have watched the spread of immorality among the lower classes consequent on the barrack system. At first the married negro who was employed in crop time on a plantation left his wife in San Fernando or other place where he had a cottage, returning to his home on Saturday night and leaving it again on Monday morning. Thus the husband and wife were parted for a week, and too often formed other relations. Mutual support and comfort existed no longer, the moral tie was broken and it was clear that marriage was a useless unmeaning clog which it is no shame to omit. From the estates the curse has spread to the towns. It is a more profitable investment to build barracks and let single rooms in them than to build detached cottages: and unmarried men and unmarried women occupy in this manner whole ranges of rooms. On plantations the demoralization is carried as far as it can go. The absentee proprietor is not there to witness the scandals. The overseers will tell you, as I have often been told by them, that they are put there to make sugar and not to look after the morals of coolies. The owner in England compares notes with other absentees and expects his crop to be made at the lowest rate. As to the means, that matters not to him. The overseer holds his situation subject to twenty-four or forty-eight hours' notice and to escape losing his place and consequent beggary he must have but one object in view: that of screwing the most he can out of his bondsman.

This lengthy quote above describes a situation of complete neglect on the part of the British administration in Trinidad. Conditions for Indians were little better in other Caribbean territories. The government of India investigated the conditions of Indian immigrants in Trinidad, as well as three other British colonies and Suriname in 1913. They found that the Indian population was infected with hookworm, malaria, and other illnesses. Given the living conditions described in the barracks in which Indians lived, such illnesses are not surprising. Treatment for such illnesses was also very poor as well. In British Guiana, it was often the case that doctors that were in charge of estate hospitals would certify that sick indentured laborers were fit for labor, even if that was not the case.

Not surprisingly, such deplorable situations often led to resistance on the part of the exploited Indians. Eric Williams points out that one tactic which was used by indentured Indians was to feint being sick to avoid work:

> [T]he indentured Indian immigrant resorted to the only weapon at his command - passive resistance. He simply malingered, or pretended to be sick, or went into the hospital. Some positively alarming statistics of the man-days lost in hospital are available for the West Indies. In French Guiana, in the first six months of 1875, where the indentured immigrants averaged 350 a month, the man-days worked numbered 26,852, and the man-days lost in hospital 26,602; the average number of days worked by each immigrant was twelve per month, while, for every day worked, one day was spent in the hospital. In Trinidad, in 1895,

for 10,720 Indian immigrants, there were 23,688 admissions to hospitals. Thus each Indian went at least twice a year to the hospital, at the expense of the planter and the government.

Cultural differences also contributed to misunderstanding and prejudice. Indians retained many elements of their languages, religions (Hinduism and Islam), and family structures, which were often portrayed as alien by the Christianized African population. Meanwhile, Indians viewed the Afro-Trinidadian lifestyle as morally lax and overly influenced by Western customs. Colonial authorities exploited these stereotypes to prevent unified labor or political movements that could challenge their power.

The controversy created by Brother Marvin's song demonstrated that building a cohesive multiracial society must not be done at the expense of diminishing the history of one group. This is an issue that goes beyond Brother Marvin's song, however. Too often diversity has meant ignoring the particular needs and concerns of black people. Mutabaruka, another musician, raised this point when he noted that Jamaica's slogan about "one people" was accurate because in Jamaica it was only "one people" who struggled; black people. This is also the same problem with Brazil's national myth about "racial democracy." It is a myth which was used to mask the racism against black people in Brazil.

www.ingramcontent.com/pod-product-compliance
Lightning Source LLC
Chambersburg PA
CBHW051656250726
48653CB00007B/2697